The Golden Years of British
STEAM TRAINS

C OLIN G ARRATT
ON THE WORK OF
T HE R EV. A.W.V. M ACE

MILEPOST

This edition first published 1995 by Milepost Publishing in conjunction with
Arcturus Publishing Limited, for Bookmart Limited.
Desford Road, Enderby, Leicester LE9 5AD

Milepost Publishing is a division of Milepost 92½.
Milepost 92½ is Colin Garratt's Audio Visual, Production, Presentation and Photographic Service for the
Railway Industry incorporating The Railway Picture Library.

Designed by Milepost and wilson design associates
Originated, Printed and Bound in the UK by Gresham Print Group, Nottingham.

ISBN 1 900193 05 1

Milepost 92½
Newton Harcourt
Leicestershire
LE8 9FH
Tel 0116 259 2068

MILEPOST

Previous page
Summer Saturday scene at Bala Junction with a Class 43XX, 2-6-0 hauling a Paddington to Pwllheli train. A Class 22XX,
0-6-0 stands with two coaches at the head of the branch to Blaenau Festiniog. One suspects that Arthur Mace has left his
case on the platform - even though it is attracting attention, it does not bear the stigma of unattended baggage these days.

INTRODUCTION

Presenting the work of the Rev. A.W.V. Mace is a joy and a privilege. Arthur Mace was born in 1908 and died in 1986; his earliest pictures date before the grouping of 1923 and he remained active as a railway photographer almost until his death. His remarkable photographic legacy, which consists of thousands of negatives embracing many sizes - both cellulose and glass plate - is now under the custodianship of Milepost 92½. The collection is being catalogued and prepared for storage in archivally safe materials.

Arthur Mace is one of a handful of individuals who have left us with a permanent vision of a past age. He was a great stylist, a great opportunist and equally at home photographing railway topography as the trains themselves.

Arthur Mace's pictures are much more than nostalgic images of a bygone age for they reveal the railway in all its dynamism in those heady days when it was the nation's principal transport system. Herein lies an essential point, for I believe that what Arthur Mace shows is the right system and that our change to a road based economy has been detrimental to the well-being of society. This book contains pictures of a viable working railway; if so magnificent a transport system could be operated with steam, how much easier it would be in today's computerised world to run an efficient modern railway fully capable of handling the nation's transport needs.

In 1939 there were 184 Dean Goods 0-6-0's in service. At the end of 1945 this total was reduced to 61, mainly through commandeering by the War Department - some being left in France after the Dunkirk evacuation. Here, we see No. 2572 heading a Pwllheli to Ruabon train on the 12th August 1935. This engine survived until 1952.

INTRODUCTION

Unlike its three rival companies, the Great Western - which dated back to the 1830s - retained its identity and absorbed a range of smaller constituent railways, principally in South Wales with such companies as the Taff Vale and Rhymney.

Locomotive development was therefore a continuous process which evolved logically throughout the nineteenth century and continued to do so until nationalisation in 1948.

Whereas the climax of motive power development occurred during the 1930s/40s in the other companies, the Great Western's final phase began at the beginning of the century with Churchward's 4-6-0 Saints and Stars. These formed a bedrock for the remainder of the company's existence and ensured a high degree of standardisation. The Saints gravitated to the Halls; the Stars to the Castles; and the Castles to the Kings.

Apart from being generic, the Great Western's locomotives were extremely handsome ; nineteenth century designs were characterised by outside frames, whilst the twentieth century ones had a very modern business like appearance. Brass chimney bands and safety valves, glorious brass number plates and name plates, green locomotives and brown and cream coaching stock endeared the railway to the general public and enthusiasts alike. It's long tradition of superb engines attracted a cult following and it was the most passionately loved of the Big Four group.

At nationalisation, the Great Western handed over 3,857 locomotives covering 60 principal classes with much of this diversity representing the tail end of the legacy inherited from the smaller absorbed railways.

Previous spread
End of the line in every sense - 0-6-0PT No. 3725 takes water at Bromyard shortly before closure in September 1964. Until 1952, the line had continued on as far as Leominster. The engine did not long outlive the branch, being withdrawn in January of 1965.

Modified Hall Class 4-6-0 No. 7905 "Fowey Hall" stands at Penzance Station with the 6.40 p.m. mail train to Paddington.

War Department Austerity 2-8-0 No. 90363 heads a freight train through the Brunel designed station at Culham between Didcot and Oxford.

King Class No. 6026 "King John" in double chimney form, stands at Shrewsbury with the Cambrian Coast Express from Paddington. The train will be worked forward from this point by smaller engines.

Hawksworth 0-6-0PT No. 8487 stands at the buffer stops of Paddington's platform 1 having brought empty stock from Old Oak Common for a down express.

Busy scene at Birmingham Snow Hill as 4-6-0 No. 6854 "Roundhill Grange" enters on an up excursion. Sadly, this fine station was closed and demolished in 1972 and only in recent years has a small substitute appeared for local services.

Bound for Ruabon and the Midlands, 2-6-0 No. 6311 crosses the Mawddach Estuary on the approach to Barmouth Junction having followed the coast from Dovey Junction to Morfa Mawddach.

Opposite
1400 Class 0-4-2T No. 5811 bowls a two coach train along the scenic branch from Bala to Blaenau Festiniog.

Tyseley based 0-6-0PT No. 3625 emerges from the stygian gloom of the tunnel and runs light into Birmingham Snow Hill Station.

Another light engine movement in the form of 0-6-0PT No. 4671 caught standing at Severn Tunnel Junction Station.

The Castle Class 4-6-0's were overwhelmingly named after castles although some earls, a few notable people and famous aircraft of the R.A.F. were also commemorated as in this picture showing Reading based No. 5076 "Gladiator".

Previous spread
The Mayflower - 8.30 a.m. Plymouth to Paddington - made its first stop at Exeter St. David's where it is seen arriving behind a King Class 4-6-0.

Severn Tunnel based Churchward 2-8-0 No. 2826 drifts slowly beside bridge engineering works.

On a wet day at Shrewsbury No. 7823 "Hook Norton Manor" heads the down Cambrian Coast Express.

A double chimney King leaves Paddington in December 1962 with a down express for Wolverhampton.

A Hawksworth County Class 4-6-0 makes a business like departure from Penzance with the up Cornishman.

Tyseley based 0-6-2T No. 5647 heads a West Midlands freight train. Two hundred of these freight hauling tanks were built between 1924 and 1928 primarily for service throughout the vast coalfields of South Wales.

Opposite page
A Churchward Class 43XX, 2-6-0 heads the Hastings to Birkenhead through train amid the outer suburbs of Birmingham.